Best Indie Books of 2019: "Pearson                    ...ut poetry collection scours littoral and urban landscapes... Vastly panoramic and deeply introspective... A startlingly intuitive new poet—one to watch."

– *Kirkus Reviews*

"stunningly reflective... Tom Pearson fills each page with an abundance of evocative language."

– JR Mercier, *Online Book Club*

"Breathtaking and engaging... Tom Pearson dances with language... The poems touch on something ubiquitous, yet untouchable... The use of language is imaginative yet precise and powerful."

— Amazon Reader Review

"Pearson's debut collection of intimate poetry offers a meditative selection of free-form vignettes across intertwining themes... Above all, Pearson demonstrates a mastery of imagery."

– *BookLife*, by *Publisher's Weekly*

Please turn the page for more reviews...

"*The Sandpiper's Spell* feels like an homage to the fragility of life. Death so close, but beauty closer. It requires slow, deep, repeated reading. The imagery is complex and layered. Often unexpected, like a dance, a quick shift in direction."

"Beautiful and haunting... moves you into a soft trance, where the poetry is no longer just made of words. It becomes an immersive experience for all the senses."

"... a pastiche of meditative vignettes and fragmented memory."

"Gorgeous use of language... leaves you with big takeaways."

The Sandpiper's Spell

**ALSO BY TOM PEARSON**

*Still, the Sky*

# THE SANDPIPER'S SPELL

*poems*

# TOM PEARSON

RANSOM POET | NEW YORK

Published by Ransom Poet Publishers (Ransom Poet LLC), New York.

Cover art and design by Owen Gent

Interior design by Tom Pearson

The Sandpiper's Spell/ Tom Pearson. -- Second Edition: April 2022
ISBN 979-8-4296898-3-8 (paperback)

Library of Congress Control Number: 2022934196

RANSOM POET PUBLISHERS
NEW YORK| RANSOMPOET.COM

# Contents

III.

IV.

# V.

The Sandpiper's Spell (Part 5)     77

VI.

The Sandpiper's Spell (Part 6)    107

VII.

The Sandpiper's Spell (Epilogue)    125

*There are some things you learn best in calm, and some in storm.*

— Willa Cather

# The Sandpiper's Spell

# Invocation

dreams and illusions
currencies of the old world
now closed for repairs

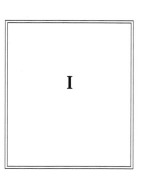

I

# The Sandpiper's Spell
Part 1

the marauders of dawn
veer along shore
where a waning tide has left
a crescent of cooler sand

the hard pan makes
for swift advance
and the trail discernible
a band now drunk
on its own velocity

appetite propels them onward
to the facing beaches
where the Atlantic
gathers at the corners
of Salt Run

waters of the Ancient City
Anastasia and the inlet
mingle with the River of Blood

   Matanzas

on nor'easterly winds
winter's tempest has washed ashore
tragedy with treasure

   and lovers lost

while mating in moonlight

   ambushed

buffeted about

shells cracked
the soft sweet meat
   of a midnight feast

carnage left strewn across a sand pile
a half claw or back leg of ghost crab
picked apart by early risers

I shadow trident footprints
chasing the dawn over dunes
stalking sideways-listing foam chasers

our silence overtaken by the
uproar of seagulls
a sphere of white down
and a daybreak of fluff

the realm of night crawlers
   foreclosed
bleached now by daylight
under the assault

   of wind

      and flight

   and trumpets

# Sunday School

in a rusted churchyard
the lawnmower blade rests
its ancient recitations
carved on cinderblock

overtaken with weeds
this sidelit ofrenda
rises above a waiting grave

   children pulled aside

flames held to fingers
taught the eternal
temperament of hell

   and self-blame

snakehandled
my cousin
rushed to the hospital
for loss of faith

   speaking in tongues

at the revival luncheon
cottonmouths slither into
a neighboring ditch

   we go down to the river

# High Chaparral

your valiant vaquero
looks back with serpentine smile
overgrown of underbrush

   a prodigal father

he sits on a barstool
at the High Chaparral
and orders a traveler

   whisky and tea

unfastened
   out-running

too much

   too...

it rolls off again
your criticism of him
this tired cowboy

   and indecision?

the war within him
until nothing left but boots
on a rain barrel

# Vanishing Point

Georgia sunset
the calico corona of
autumn forgetfulness

Helios melts red into clay

clouds of frenzied gnats
a quivering vertigo
of distant laughter

orange evangelist
the summer he rode into town

headlights piercing the hill
rounding red road in twilight

covered in white now

   a vanishing point

windblown shawls
moss women caught in storm
draped over live oak

bales of hay
cast shadows in moonlight

   the dearly departs

# Fledgling

past quarrels furnish
all the rooms back home

    from the driveway

a fisherman in waders
bisects the horizon
moving slowly over mudflats

    an engine revving

disheveled by water spouts
cattails in the marsh
mark barometric oppression

    dirt road turns to dust

cardinals shake bedheads
and scatter droplets
onto hibiscus petals

    past the county line

on Tolomato Road
dragonflies ride air currents
over the truck hood

# Circus World

two veiled by greasepaint
inside a rain pool's reflection
faces look back
from steaming pavement

   a misplaced summer

jokers in June
still unknown to the other
and the smiling specter of a third

   evaporating in a midday haze

on a back corner of childhood
the tree we climbed and stayed
   past dark

then a secret that opened a door

   the next morning
     slammed shut

his silhouette by the ditch
near Grace at the end of 5th

we were not the only ones
to vanish here

   among the losses of the Eighties

and I've forgotten what you
looked like then
your face painted

forever framed

persisting in Polaroid

hidden beneath the rouge
and powder

sick from the rollercoaster
I was too afraid to ride

when mice ruled the land

and we were hand

in hand

in hand

now each night
farther from truth it travels

you who kissed me
hard on the mouth

when we were both ten

Circus World gone too
like so many things after
the orange blossom groves

## Boxing

looming larger than the man
   distorted
but glorious

ready as desire

distance looks backward
burrowing tunnels
through self

   in the second dimension

flatlanders
dwelling in lamplight

   lolling in rocking chairs

life in profile's past
an inch never more
in one plane

   traveling in projection

with wavering semaphore
   his hidden history plays
in contours on the wall

# Gallery Opening

prisoners
for showcasing

   personae enframed

this superficial mold
holds us tightly
inflates with accolades
spilling over
the meaning of our madness
lost in consumption

   criticism and praise

withering in misrecognition

hidden within
these narrow margins
   of acceptance and rejection

ideas displayed
before a panel
of predators

   let the feast begin

II

# The Sandpiper's Spell
Part 2

Porpoise Point up ahead
in the coquina deposits a mermaid's purse

black leathery diablo with whiskers
and sand along its seams
a swollen and pregnant belly

   inside
      emergent life

ready to meet the incoming tide
and unfold itself to the waiting world

   the progenitor's hope

then more purses nested in the sea rack
draped with sargassum boas
shining along a new shoreline

the curtained perimeter of a wall
nightly eroded
the previous day's work made and re-made

I throw purses back into the water
along my way
   starfish too

already this is a morning
   of too many funerals

# Fish Stories

the fisherman's wife
sits unhappy on her throne
   go ask the flounder


the fisherman's knife
iridescent scales in flight
   a midnight rainbow


the fisherman's catch
pressed for too much mystery
   rides a roiling sea

## Three Wishes

one wish for myself
one more for those expecting
   something of myself


the space needed to
battle these expectations:
   two wishes granted


to those now waiting
who wish something of us still:
   a need to finish

## Night Journey

sage salientian
who bounds awake in two worlds
brings to him amphibious sleep

a bed made just right
for a psyche's hospitality
to the tempest-tossed traveler

   vacancy

it comes on dark wind
sets consciousness in motion
with a blessing and a curse

towers of masquerade windows
curtains open on false faces
nightlight shining on oak

the finality of the topside world
not the same as in this dream

where he relives it nightly
upon down pillows

   banishment

the pigeon's reflection watches
as his shadow walks him into town
light cracking stone

toy soldiers stand guard
press forward

a doll looks the other way

exiles all

the seaside fortress sleeping
soundly now
and for a season more

on his night journey
croaking anuras
ring out through the swamp

the somnambulist's
restful promenade
glides along a feathered vane

sleeping his sleep

   walking his walk

until the time is right

   to wake again

## Creation

orbiting droplets
earth pearl spinning in saddle shell
an ocean of heaven

   one: red sky at morning

Okeanos rides forth
a leviathan on seafoam
with titanic arms encircling
mingles his salt with Tethys

into marsh and canopied hammock

he calls out the first ahoy
running clear
sawing Atlantis
severing the anchor of seven seas

   two: red sky at night

her naked body
like a wisp of smoke rising
a red glazed genie

moon sleeve for sunlight
day fitting into evening
star sky holds them both

   and it was good

# Awakening

one covers the bed
an incisive prediction
his innocence lost

the other rules slumber
and cuts his hair with a knife
blinding the mighty

charging into dark
Samson with a flashlight
comes falling down stairs

   an interloper banished

on a backlit heaven
spiral staircase at dawn
backdoor to yonder world

   opens

shedding light into
darkest rooms on darkest nights

   walls crumbling

his torch leading
to power reclaimed
that which needs protection
now loyal to itself

# Hephaestus

metal to flesh
the handsome laborer priest
fashioning in exile

influencing heat
his calloused hands disappear
behind a steam veil

palms that clench and release
hold wide possibility
to shape and to frame

beneath his garment
white and soft with fine dark hairs
forming rivers onto maps

the pneumatic gift
he offers from injury
to fabricate life

his limp retraction
still falling in memory
never hitting the ground

# Observation

the pressure to create
under the watchful eye
of the gorgon

the stone-cold
scrutiny of uninspiration

dust

   to dust

      to dust

III

# The Sandpiper's Spell

Part 3

the twilight infantry
that leaves
the battlefield of daybreak
a shell of upturned ocean
remains in shadow

but I know those I follow
the ground patrol
that scurries out
as the periwinkles burrow

bubbling hollows
in retracting water

small pinkish white birds

   sand-piping their way
along shore

over the next dune
coming to rest in a salted city
that ran aground in the night

   a waking tide pool

trap of enchantment

sand bars
that make archipelagos

beyond the breakers

   warnings of drop off

careful wading

past the jetties
onto the more
gradual descent
of the North River

on higher ground
the puddles warm
the shoals soft

a relief from
the curves of coquina crust
that cut the bottoms
    of my feet

orangebluegreenpurple
    shells
cast a snaky mosaic
over the upper dunes

and there they wait

black diamonds

    arrowheads of the ocean

the teeth of the ancient ones

hammerheads
and megalodons
    tiger
        lemon
    and sand sharks

makos and bulls

found with the gift
of concentration

allotted
   only
to the lonely

for those who hide
within themselves
hoping to go
unnoticed

   who notice
      everything

here in the wake of winter
talismans of transformation

to use in the alchemy of spring

## Childhood

ants make their way up

   on
      and over

mapping the
subterranean hollows all
our lives were built upon

the trailer
off its cinderblocks
with prow pointing forward
hitches to the back
of the reaper truck

   our childhood
      hauled to the city dump

still hanging in a corner
a netless basketball hoop
its snuff lip
drooping to one side

the trees outlive
our imagination here

the owl lamp
the black leather sofa
a t-shirt in rags
used to wipe down
counter tops

the propane tank
our makeshift steed

resting in its corral

    they watch

dumbfounded to see us

    here

standing beside
    our own names
misspelled in asphalt

that historic moment of progress
that paved over our dirt beginnings

the treehouse
and the mute girl
always taller than the rest

J gone in the night
D dispersing in daylight

Z in the ground
beyond the ravines

and the loblollies and oaks
inside the fence line

    taken in

to make room for a new lot

while the grandmothers
and grandfathers
hold the perimeter

the live oaks and maples
pines and palmettos

witches hair and
conquistadors beards
caught in their branches

still protecting what remains
of us in their scared shadows

even in their misgivings
and judgements for what
we've squandered

such spiritual derelicts

running upwind in
this death coat

    unravelling

## Lost Boys

the lost boys
of Lower Matecumbe
stare at the cola tins

    rattling on the walls

amplifying the
downward pull of
nightly rhythms

synonymous desire
blazing through
unappreciative audiences

    infects me

a guitar resting on his knee

    waiting

       nervously

in that dimly lit corner
of the Islamorada

    nightly smoldering

me wishing to go unnoticed
you trilling melancholy breezes
across a smoky room

    the lyrics trite:

*a waning moon
on an embittered*

*and white-sanded shore*

punishes with its
sentimentality

*into the salt night*
*of marshmallow breakers*

this sentimentality
recorded for posterity
threw a rock
at the ocean

   and wrote it
again in the sand

held hands laughing

   watching it all wash away

# Nombre de Dios

*for Jimmy*

among these few
   small wonders

straddled by moss
the heavy breath of summer
presses down upon our backs

in my own obscure necropolis
the ghosts of Spanish soldiers
walk cobblestone streets

a breeze climbs the
   hill from the bay

it rustles the palms
   that fan my thoughts

beneath Saint Francis
whispering salvation among the ruins

   a sister shutters out the gray

pealing mission bells
Her shrine darkened by showers
thunder claps in storm skies

royal orchids bow
in the presence of summer rain
court now in session

shuddering discard
two missiles drop from above
the peacock's tail feathers

thatched roof rustling

altar rocking
holy water glistens on the floor

winds of Dora
torches of Drake

   the city once again usurped

extinguished velas
broken stain glass crucifix
the pulse of a blazing citadel

   in shrouded sunset

cardinals flicker
a canopy of red
illuminating a distant beacon

its great cross towering over
an omniscient reminder
of ancestral footsteps

   silence

     and a squirrel

sit ceremoniously on a grave

# Tourist

two tempests later

rays of a light ceremony
converge through glass upon
quivering leaves

sparks a burning point

hot and bright
and invisible

learns to strike hard

   strike fast

     strike first

while on a barstool
in the shallows she sits
facing inland as the tides
rise around her warnings

he looks away
as the trolley stops

then the tour ends
and we all step out from
last season's contamination

## Souvenirs

our conversation
carries us far into dark
the mosquitos feast

    morning

nothing left to say
we watch an egret
stalk a fisherman

    along the span of a season

and this pier

    the cannons fire

evening oysters spit their
objections to the outgoing tide

    a chorus of disapproval

bayonets in the sky
drop moon beams between
yellow yucca leaves

these shiny souvenirs
nails made in the blacksmith's forge
seal yesterday shut

IV

# The Sandpiper's Spell

Part 4

some I give to the
glassblower woman
to fashion necklaces for the
*touristas*

but the tiny black teeth
I keep for myself
   homeward
       pocketful
   and carefully carted

hidden in the water heater panel

a mason jar
   nestled behind
the wall of a bedroom closet

   brimful

and stretched over top
with sackcloth
and rubber band

secured beneath
metal rim topper

contents of blazing ebony fire
indestructible life-force
from a great dead ancestor

Holy Predator!
O Most Precious Relics!

Those Which Replenish and

Rend Nourishment
from the Briny Deep!

these for keeping
along with a container
of pine pollen
gathered from the yard

catkins that drop
from a neighbor's tree

## Far-sighted

a great grandmother
rises over East Williamsburg

somewhere beyond
Our Lady Guadalupe

painted on a roll gate
near Bushwick Avenue

an orange paper lantern giantess

bending herself
around street corners
a silent voice among the shouting

the last guest to arrive to the party

she lowers herself
to rock me to sleep
in this place of my own making

a reminder of another time
back home
    surrounding us
her long gray hair flowing
behind her failing eyesight

blindly fingering her way
through the open yard

## Patience

army tanks
resting on one hip
sink into the tall grass

by the playground
mothers hunt
for hypodermic needles
among dandelions

their children crying
from car seats
ready to run
into these minefields

   meanwhile

the stone boy
never moves
from the shore's edge

his pole cast cross river

waiting to hook a dream

## Story Lodge

she speaks it piping hot
hard truth served
like buttered grits

whether we pray
in His name or Yours
Creator knows
when and where
to RSVP

meet us later
at Granny's

after eviction from
the Broken Arrow Trailer Park
where they all pray
in Jesus's name
but pay
in Jackson's image

there's a vacancy sign
near a wrong turn
at Birdtown
by two beavers
fighting over a fat log

(at the end of Drama Road)

all of us so far from home

the billboard up ahead
missing a corner
and a *.com*

but I make out *twofeathers*
and scroll for info

this domain up for sale
like all the rest around here

then follow the river
into lateness of afternoon

water strider's invisible feet
casts a butterfly's shadow
on the mud bottom of
a mountain stream

translucent lily pads
at the ends of spindly legs
walk on bright light water
a Jesus bug in sunshine

standing pine
standing tall
still standing
pine tall

star boys in the sky
all seven of us together again
lost here tonight

by the freshly cut
sweetgrass side road
now in deepest midnight

where time ran off
in drain ditches
in the fast lane of a water flow

fancy dancing
torrents
downstream

and thoughts slowly
combing through
rock mosses
brushing hair in moonlight

friendly fire
a fallen tree
a casualty
in the wake of beaver's
fight for territory

asks the primordial question:

in which corner of the darkness
will I make my home?

trees lay long like fingers
pointing a way into the night

always down now
forward
and down

a cover of blackness
offering safe passage

across

pilgrims leaving
quiet
at river's edge
teardrops
and quiet

laying down
troubles
on the prison side

give away
clear away
give
clear
seven rounds
we go

me and the night

the injury
I give to the mountain
and to the log wolf
or is it a log bear?
as sun and mist
raise the morning

how long have we been
in all this time
resting in
the ability to stand winter

heart wood to hard wood?

the center holding tight
our lives growing
from unknown edges
always something to protect

a quiet god's misty whispers
a living leaf on a dying branch
an offspring standing alone

the single pine atop Mingo Falls
the only pine in these piney hills

and the seventh boy
forged in fire

the lonely evergreen
atop the falls
springing forth

from scarification
in the Thunderlands

germination
(newness)
a clearing way

first changing leaf of new autumn
the rusty top
and burnt crisp halo
of life's zenith

and a son searching
reaching higher
arms outstretched to fire

yellow tears
falling from sky vault
cover the river in a quilt

and my distant boys
of distant galaxies

six to one and flame to flame
flicker here
all together again

in the conifer-scented season
of declining day

## Sin Eaters

claws of the anima
stretching in sunlight

an inopportune
arrival meets sharpened knife
after sleep surprise

hacked to death
twitching
the gentleman caller
dismissed

wardrobe apartment
a doorman for skeletons
in tall tower town

food for predator
the innocent visitor
knocks on candy doors

   beards turn blue

she knits herself home
the cat chasing her ribbons
as red apples fall

their manly hearts
food for carrion

## Death of a...

just ask the lonely

waiting by the roadside
a scale of balance

suitcase in each hand

the thin man
next to me

nothing to tether him
steps into the street

a distant saxophone
blows suicide notes

## Day Dreams

the captain's log

written on mud paths
stamped by steam shoes
black smoke stacks
walking storm seas

the unlaced navigator
takes the wheel in rain

over a milky ocean
nourishment flees
on sugary life boats

   two-by-two

as the flood recedes
from his narrative arc
Noah waits for news

no ravens or doves this dawn

flight flutters
forever forgotten

white bubbles button
his fish face
to his man body

   an inverted voyeur

the bleached bones
of his ship
wrecked

an actor
   once upon a time

some small parts
on 1970s television

ambition
washed ashore
on this island

his messages
daily sent
bottles
lost down dish drains

on the other side of his
forgetfulness and melancholy

   an expatriated daydream

sitting in the same cafe
on the beach at the edge of a cliff

daily
wondering if his dog
will outlive him

# Bedtime Story

so cold
our synthetic blankets
setting off lighting
beneath the sheets
and sparks
along the ceiling

twenty-seven degrees

the bath drawn
muddy and warm

running from the silverfish
that Granny called centipedes

to burn our butts
on the furnace

later

summer

so hot
our ice boxed sheets
lay over us

under floor fans with hands
waving palm fronds
at sticky brows

breathing in cigarette smoke
and cat hair

trying not to drown in our
own puddles

of forever

even now
the endless nights

shadows rise
to catch the light

together

they pass one another
like former lovers
now just friends
meeting in the sky

with all the years in between

my sheep
    counting

me

## Asleep

18-wheelers resting
beyond the runway
white puppies

muzzles jutting
on a carpet of asphalt
wheelpaws tucked
beneath fat bellies

where mountains of gray mist
and rolling moss hills
give way to retracting landing gear

a colony of diminishing dump trucks
serving a merciless queen
all streak yellowish

through a Stepford hive

from the roar of thrusting engines
waking from a daydream
of a clone world
shrinking now

below an obfuscating cloud cover

# Home

ascent from the pink room
on a blue velvet dusk
a window to the world opens
on a ravaged dumpster

the voice of Kerouac
and the accent of a fading
New York
the cadence of longing
for the loss of loss

freedom in one of its guises

no use for grief laid down

in the waters of Mingo Falls
on the ridge of the Dragon's Back
in the corn snow of St. Mary's Glacier

leveling off

and momentarily
what matters most
passes on a cumulus

in this place of peace
at thirty thousand feet

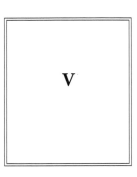

V

# The Sandpiper's Spell

Part 5

back from shore
the landscape surveyed from
the red cedar picnic table

   safe from Misty

with a bird's eye view
of the trailer park

spotting catkins in clusters
plotting a course

   gathering rapidly

before she catches the scent
of my intentions

running cluster to cluster
and back to table
waiting until her interest
wanes

   and my bag is full

atop the table
husking pods
breaking off beaks
sliding grain
down stalks
until each is left
naked
   brown
and twisted

the grain
siloed in a tobacco tin

waiting for the right moment
for a witch moon
to creep over the canopy

then with teeth held close
and grain sprinkled
in a penumbra around me

from the song sung
in the fullness of moon
over the bones
of what washed ashore

   a new cycle

      slowly spinning

   quickening

      born...

above our bed
snow gathers on the skylight
white upon my grave

overlooking
the road
we took to get here

the villages
left standing

after fire failed

the east side
of the fortress wall
thrusts its chin
to a forgetful wind

past the point
where he could reach

I did not push him
but I lured him just the same

a quarter inch between
capture or release

now

on this drowsy road
a lonely dragon
coils himself
carefully to sleep

sky gondola floats the traveler
beyond the horizon
of now knowing

monastery emerges
from mists atop a mountain

the bamboo bends low
   in greeting

circular recognition
amid the din of white faces

I dream of kumquats

the sky overcast
with meringue

throws shadows on silk

fog lifting

    today in motion
        undomesticates us

for this perfect moment
one drop in a clepsydra
now waiting to fall

under storm sky reflections
a village of umbrellas
repositions me

winter's miracle
on a road
back to self
a red flower

blooms

her shadowbox veil
blue sun sky wheel

turns

a cathedral rises

water-colored day
domes of onion
in the sky

   open

through rain

we move through cities
with poems
   in pockets

bristles of horsehair
in our open mouths
keep us from choking

with red on our hands
we make sacred this garment
red upon our heads

clay of deep earth
upon us and our likeness
hurry before rain

received by damp earth
saguaros sweetly sleeping
a Phoenix landing

this covert dream

beads your
   face on a feather

a thought to wear
around my neck

while this muse
hunts by night
and all that needs creation
by morning is done

surfacing now
the overburden gone

a perfectly placed rain
follows sideways

strip-mining
the mountain

clouds above Rockies
an angel hood ornament
spreads its wings in flight

outside the circle
a water sprinkler's rainbow
color comes and goes

nestled deep
in this vinyl-sided cavern
a sibyl in enemy territory

riding on easterly winds
overturning
prognostications
in doorways

no rewrites

taking dictation
as it were
from
a fast-talking god

running out of ink
and oak leaves

blowing up troubles
leeward in late season
a tipping point past equinox

time running out
on daylight

getting shorter with age

collecting
books
and pens
and paper

for the
  journey

underground

Sunny Jim's and
God's Country Cowboy Church
into Eden Valley

on the lotus lake
Sister Mary Juniper
ripples forth a prayer

an overflowing
  wellspring

this
empty

bowl

VI

# The Sandpiper's Spell

Part 6

... a new cycle

    slowly spinning

quickening

    born...

by the psychic side door
   waiting
into a labyrinth
   the forest comes
      surrounding

standing
   growing upward
      growing outward
opening between the trunks
passages of exfoliating bark

red orange pine needles
cross hatching the ground

pollen pods
   and branches dividing
      cluster by cluster

pulled up and back
lifted upon a first flight

bright burnt umber
   loblolly loblolly loblolly
above its canopy

aerial view drops down

   onto table top

Misty waiting

we go
   up steps
the trailer's back door
   on cinderblocks

an old bedroom
(an open wall)
   back closet hot water heater
hides atomic marble
a sun shining brightly

     into reversal
   rewind
forward
and back on a single tear

time passing

   slowly
     and sickly

and slowly again

(richer and more lonesome
than before)

and then

doors that open
along grassy edges

on the rind
of a green knoll

    walk-float

edgeways peel downward
    throwing squares into spiral
      with conical endpoints
    a vortex

billowing off the edges
    and through center

parachuting
    to surface
dropping
    through bottom

onto spongy
moss-covered nothingness

    shifting

jagged frenzied
    parallelograms
moving mountains
    thwarting vision

steadying against
the feet of the giant
clasping each
    fingers to toes
holding Self

made larger

snake-like with head in clouds
and yester skin falling away

shedding
previous seasons

   compressing the remains
      into new world

taken in one hand
and Misty in the other

I expect fire
but it is air that comes

forming
from hazy geometry
     to bring us up through center
   back to surface
on an easy breeze

with the third
prescription
and final ingredient

in the ceremony of
   blue world
     under yellow sun
in the palm of fourth hand

pollen grain
and shark's teeth

   now a marble spinning

moving upward
into forbearance

billowing outward
into forgiveness

to the seventh direction

on a gentle wind

## Returning

safe passage cast
behind the tail feather
of the dove in flight

crossing

between the crashing rocks

need you tonight
under a false ceiling
and the smell of chicken
frying across the street

permeates this labyrinth

dawn has come
no matter how long
we try to pretend the night

walking home

the morning murmuration
starlings rotate the sky

a welcome sight

in this city

    remembering

# Ouroboros

blinded by our own metaphor
our inability to see in the dark
because we've put up these many lights

on a street cloaked in brightest invisibility
the shimmering letters
of the billboard read

   *fountain of youth*

glittering gold in the headlights
another corner turned

looming brown above the eaves
crescent pouring water
into the dipper under a
blanket of sky sparklers

   a sky chasing its tail

on a dilapidated balcony
a broken campaign sign reads only

   *Make America...*

those that grow low surviving
the too-tall destroyed

the aftermath of another storm

# Truce

crowned over
violet waters vast
golden throne too small

anchors drop on sandy shores
the heart of the ocean
with gills collapsed
beached here
suffocating

on a blue green dawn
these paper lantern people
float cautiously
through open portholes

the ruinous face
studying its salt water reflection

by the tall teeth grass
and sea oat dunes
the elders speak to the young

growing pains measured
sentences commuted

a momentary truce in the war
with the place
from whence we came

# Glow

in a hand-held mirror
the space cowboy
finds an angel's face

his narrow waist
a cactus squeezed for water
parched in dry season

he stilt-walks the night
a net high in the heavens
catching star splinters

bleaching his bones
in sky light

sanitizing leftover dreams

the rough sound of
metal scrubbers
scouring porcelain prayers

# Sistrum

*for Zach*

our illusions
require alibis

the real magic
easier to explain

guard down
bravely-held

talking all night
and drinking to keep
up with the conversation

finding teachings in the form

    a thirteenth moon
    year-end bonus
    this crystal lullaby

containing
the colors of the others

    and time out of mind

putting back pieces
gaining story-strength

the medicine
for paradise wounds

clearing the water
seeing to bottom

    *go go yo tay*

until we are heart-full

    again

in once-upon-a-timeness

no longer toxic
of self-venom

hateful
in withholding

now a new rattle
of experience
layered onto our backsides

able to shed
growing
holding

in this relationship
between light and shadow
it's easy to lose the way
in the darkening land

there are conjurers there
that mean harm

turning tricks
in quiet company

but it is also the land of
the thunder beings

    storming the night sky

shadows casting light

## Sunrise

gold and coin dispenser of dreams
a drive thru topless Tuesday traffic

coffee
   we go

Spokane

the teller of truth
a fire always lit
any 2AM you turn away
six cigarettes later on her freezing deck

her grandmother spilling the beans
on her deathbed:

   two doors down

living with an orange corona
headdress of hair
on top of her sleepy head
a beehive waterfall

her false eyelashes
perfectly glued
flutter above her scrawny
housecoat-clad shoulders

creating praying arousing
blowing smoke rivulets
over riveted aluminum wings

crossing another's jet stream
as they spiral into an

orange and blue parfait sunrise

half asleep on this morning
of Christmas Eve between coasts
departure splits the horizon

casting light upward
it slams back from a nimbus

    blood candy sky

sand in stone
snow on mountain
crimson salt bleeding rivers from
under the mountain's petticoat

    under us
        clouds above them
    sun above clouds
        us between the clouds
            and sun

I want to sauna
inside a coffee cup

but she brings
    a paper traveler

# Uno

*for Renata*

for the kiss that never came
crawling on thorns of faith
hot vapor over cold ground

she mouthed every word
to every song
immunizing us against
San Valentín

two sides to every passion
a cantadora crooned

through each whisper of the heel
feet navigating the terrain
of together loneliness

sangria glasses leached
the pigment from our lips
trading its own hue
on our tongues

# Hahalua

*for Carolyn*

forty below
a shrouded prism pit
bottom blue
of sable sea

sitting
waiting
they come

Two-Breaths

moving in shallows
angels gliding
over acoustic inhales
souls rising upright
on black bubbles

the wingspan of
this liminal buoyancy
between floatation and flight
on together currents

death lessons
for what is to come

one day
in the letting go

spirit breaching surface

# Guardian

remembered

   supplanting
following
of and into

the oceanic

grace hears
   clemency cast

triumphant star

a gemstone
   strong
   and singing

VII

# The Sandpiper's Spell

Epilogue

in this season of coquina

a shovel of the foot reveals
pinks and blues and beige

bivalves burying themselves
against the drying shore
under granular blankets

   waiting

to awaken

on the next rising
when high tide
will bring them home

but not yet

inspiring them to unrest
I scoop tiny clams
in radiant casings

letting them slip through my fingers
and burrow again
each time with greater urgency

   turning to greet the water
   meeting
   (consumed)

suspended

ripples running
over feet

taking the sand
away from underneath

carrying me
out
on a current

digging me
deeper into trenches

so much winterized
kissed by water's warmth

opening

receiving

blessings uttered to the horizon
the asking itself
creating the condition
sought

soles tickled
by eroding sand
and then the burden
lifts upon a rising tide

sand water realization
all this connecting

self to Self

surrounding
ceremony

shore to shore

a secret

to which nothing is witness

long after night has fallen

again

tides rise and fall on the
six and twelve and twenty-four

for every sleep I take
the coquina take two

what was in the morning
is so again in evening
back into the endlessness
of the deep

while out in the blue canyon
another channel

opens

# Cadence

amid the boundary layer winds
a flock hovers along the shoreline
and jettisons forth

I am meant to take notice
as I leave the beach

without goodbye

# Acknowledgments

This new edition of *The Sandpiper's Spell* is made possible by Third Rail Projects and Ransom Poet Publishers.

Some of the poems and stanzas have been previously published in *Poetry Quarterly*, *Haiku Journal*, *Three Line Poetry*, and other periodicals. Many of the poems like *High Chaparral* and *Vanishing Point* also contain some of the written inspirations of early theatrical projects and connect to my work in the performing arts.

Gratitude to Elizabeth Carena, Andrea Lepcio, Marilyn Morris, James Pearson, Carolyn Rhodes, and Jennifer Trice for their editorial suggestions for the first edition, and to J.T. Garrett for his teachings in the medicine way. Special thanks also to Owen Gent for the beautiful new cover design for this edition.

Deep appreciation to Dr. Clarissa Pinkola Estés and her Archetypal and Cross-Cultural Studies Institute for the inspiration to finish this volume, to sing flesh back onto the bones, and most of all, for the notion to take that which cannot be made right and to make it holy. I am forever indebted to Dr. Estés, her work, and her trainings.

Tom Pearson
New York

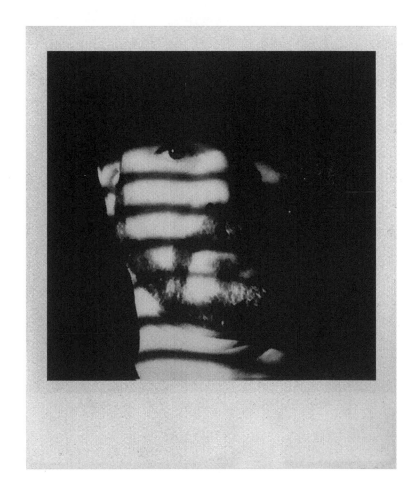

Tom Pearson, Self-Portrait, Moscow, 2018

# About the Author

Tom Pearson works in theater, dance, film, poetry and multi-media visual art. He is known for his original works for theater including the long-running, off-Broadway immersive hits *Then She Fell* and *The Grand Paradise* and as a co-founder and co-director of the New York-based Third Rail Projects and Global Performance Studio.

Tom has been named among the "100 Most Influential People in Brooklyn Culture" by *Brooklyn Magazine* and has received numerous accolades for his work including two New York Dance & Performance (BESSIE) Awards, a Kingsbury Award in writing from the Florida State University, and several international film festival awards for his collaborative experimental short film, *The Night Garden*. He has also received commissions from Lincoln Center for the Performing Arts, La Jolla Playhouse, Jacob's Pillow, Folger Shakespeare Library, Lower Manhattan Cultural Council, Danspace Project, Hong Kong Youth Arts Foundation, and more.

Tom has received fellowships and artist residencies from: CEC ArtsLink (Russia); The Bogliasco Foundation (Italy); the Center for the Arts at Wesleyan University (USA); and Olin College of Engineering (USA); among others.

He is the author of two books, *The Sandpiper's Spell* and *Still, the Sky*. More information available at his website and on social media at: tompearsonnyc.com and @tompearsonnyc.

Made in the USA
Middletown, DE
15 May 2022